£ 2.75

I0636370

£3.50

Text: by *John Kercher* Front cover photographs
Duncan Raban (All Action Photographic) Inside
photographs supplied by and are copyright
Retna Pictures Limited.

Published by

GRANDREAMS LIMITED,
Jadwin House, 205/211 Kentish Town Road,
London NW5 2JU.

Printed in Holland.

ISBN O 86227 416 8

contents

The a~ha Story

E veryone likes to know where groups get their names from and a-ha chose theirs in about as uncontrived and spontaneous a method as was possible.

"We'd tried to think up lots of things," says Pal, "and then one day Mags just said 'Aha' and we all knew instantly that it was for us.

"Not only did it sound nice and easy to say, people could remember it without any difficulty, but it almost means the same thing in practically every language in the world. That universal appeal was just what we needed and so from that day on we were a-ha."

It certainly hasn't done them any harm, and they've lived up to the element of surprise that the word conveys. But just how did the group come into being and just how tough has been their struggle to the top of the world's charts?

On the surface, it looks as if they made an overnight success, but nothing could be further from the truth. In reality, it took Morten, Pal and Mags something like four years to really get to the high plateau that they occupy today in the music business. It was a long period of frustration and sheer desperation, of living in rough conditions and just hoping. But they stuck it out, knowing that some day they'd be famous. And that paid off as every fan of the band now knows.

For a start, whilst quite a few other European countries had made their mark in the world of pop music, from places like Sweden and Germany, Norway was hardly considered to be a hive of musical activity. The population was small and as Mags says: "With fishing being the predominant industry and lots of small towns, you don't get the kind of music culture flourishing that you do in other countries."

For the real beginnings of a-ha you have to go way back into the schooldays of Pal and Mags. "We started thinking of forming a group when we were about ten years old," says Pal. "Up until then, most of the real rock'n'roll or pop music we'd heard on the radio or on record. We'd both had a classical musical upbringing until then. There weren't many Norwegian bands playing the kind of stuff that we liked."

Their tastes were predominantly for British and American groups and The Doors featured prominently in their record collections. "In fact when we first got a group together it was Beatle-ish and then later, more like The Doors," says Mags. "The music wasn't commercial at all. We didn't want to try and compromise our music like so many other bands did who were trying to get recording contracts. But we paid the price in that it didn't get us anywhere."

They made one attempt at coming to London without Morten, who stayed behind in Norway to form his own blues band. "It was just nice to be able to do something completely different for a while," he says. "I originally thought that they were just making a reconnaissance trip to London to test the water. But in fact they were already trying to make it!"

Their history shows that they didn't succeed. In fact the idea of a Norwegian band seemed a bit of a joke to most people which, is

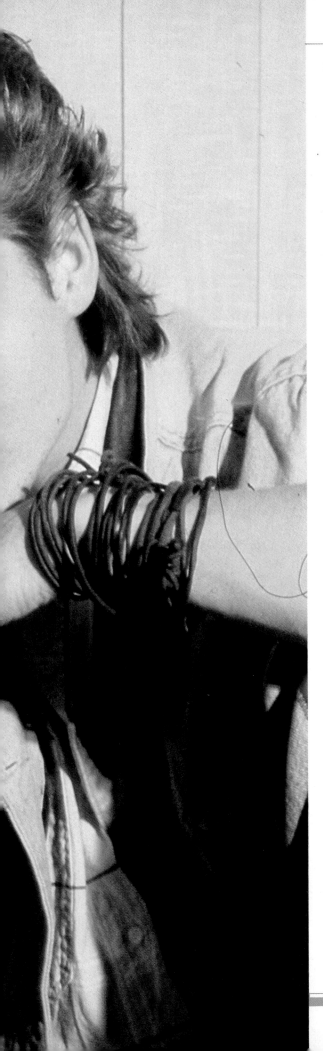

pretty unkind when you think of it. But going on what the country had so far produced no-one was interested. Pal and Mags didn't have a manager either which made things more difficult and complicated for them.

When Pal and Mags returned to Norway they were not completely disillusioned and rejoined Morten, intent on being successful the next time around. Morten says: "I think that the period that they were away was good in a way because it gave us all a chance to develop musically."

Mags agrees that the venture was not entirely fruitless. "At least we had not wasted our time in London and had had an opportunity to understand how the record business worked there. It meant that the next time we went to England we would know at least where to go." Although that didn't necessarily mean that things would be any easier for them!

It was really on their return to Norway that they chose the name a-ha and got to work on more commercial material.

Arriving in England for the second time was an equally traumatic experience. They took a small flat, of which Morten says: "It was one of the coldest places that you could imagine. If you think that Norway is cold in winter it was nothing as compared to the accommodation we had."

A lot of this discomfort was due to their lack of money. "We were scrabbling around every day trying to find the money to put into the meter to keep the electric lights on and the heater going. It was terrible. We froze." Also, trying to be creative in this kind of environment was not all that easy either. They all agree that it was often warmer outside than indoors.

Food was another problem. "We couldn't afford to go to restaurants or anything like that," says Pal. Comments range from awful meals to not even being able to afford to eat. "I've eaten some rough stuff in my time," says Mags, "but the concoctions we put together in that flat were like nothing man ever invented!"

Living together under those circumstances and in such cramped conditions also produced quite a few tensions in the band. "You really get to know someone when you are living in their pocket every hour of the day and night," says

Pal. So there were quite a few disagreements about all and everything borne out of their frustrations.

If it was anyone who held things together at that time it was probably Pal, who with his determination to succeed, driving enthusiasm and consistent hard work on the group's songs made things easier. Both Mags and Morten say that they admire him for that. But then Pal and Morten also flatter Mags in that they consider his humour as being valuable in pulling them through some of the really tough moments!

The years of hard work and trying to make it in England began to bear fruit when they eventually found themselves a manager. It was on a day when their frustrations had just about reached maximum temperature. From then on things began to look better. They became more organized with someone to give them direction, and also someone who could successfully interest the various executives at the major recording companies to come along and listen to just what the band could do.

He managed to achieve a lot in a short time and soon the group found themselves with a hired rehearsal studio ready to play for a succession of record company talent scouts. "It was a bit weird really," says Morten, "because we just played to each person as they sat there and listened and we were trying to convey the atmosphere of a live concert!" Not easy with an audience of one, but they managed to do it.

The first person to hear them was an executive from Warner Brothers, but no contract was forthcoming. Then, after being heard by almost everyone else, it was ironic, and perhaps to their advantage, that that very executive was to sign them on the American Warner Brothers label. He was impressed with their vitality and the originality of their songs and has no doubt received many a pat on the back since!

So the days when a-ha had to sleep for a couple of months on the floor of a recording studio because they had nowhere to stay were becoming a distant memory. They now had their enthusiasm fired. They had a manager and a recording deal and soon began work on an album and a single.

Most of the album, Hunting High And

Low was written by Pal, and from it was drawn their debut single, *Take On Me*. It was obvious, however, that in order to conquer the American market they had to accompany it with a superb video which would be accepted by the 24 hour video, cable, music television channel, MTV. If they could get sufficient play on that there would be a good chance that the record would sell, since the power of MTV is that great.

Just what to do presented a problem. "We always fancied the idea of doing something with animation," says Mags, "and the idea was conceived of maybe combining normal action with half animation." Steve Barron, who had become somewhat of a legend in the video marketplace was brought in and the result was that *Take On Me* zoomed into the charts.

Just how powerful the video was is illustrated by the fact that the single had been released before without any accompanying film and had not been successful. Now with powerful imagery to go with it, they achieved their ambition.

Within a short time, it rocketed to the top of the American charts. Britain followed and then practically every major chart in the world. It was more than they could have even hoped for.

Quickly, a second single was released, *The Sun Always Shines On TV*, which has enjoyed equal success. From then on, world domination was uppermost in their minds.

The group have made their base in Britain and bought homes here. It all seems such a long way from those days of living in cramped accommodation, with nothing to eat and being freezing cold. But it now seems to have been well worth it and is a tribute to their reluctance to ever give in.

Many a group might well have just thrown in the towel and gone home. But a-ha had the resilience to hold on and prove to the world that if you believe in yourself then sooner or later other people are going to believe in you and give you the chance you've been waiting for!

Just how they see themselves and their future is summed up by Pal. "We don't want to be considered as just another teeny band," he says. "We see ourselves as winning audiences from every age group!"

pal waaktaar of

a~ha

did you k

Morten is also a pop fan´ himself and one of the people he really likes to listen to is Sting!

Pal thinks that his major fault is that he can get too depressed too quickly and doesn't really like to be considered the 'moody one'.

He also says: "We want world domination of the charts."

now that....

Morten once said: "I used to fall in love too often and too quickly. I could see a girl in the street and fall head over heels in love with her."

That Mags is the really hard drinker of the group.

Morten is something of an authority on butterflies. He has books on the subject and spent many years studying them in his spare time.

did you k

The band all work hard on perfecting their English and even teach each other new words!

Pal is a very romantic guy and that when he has a girlfriend he can think of no-one else.

Mags likes surfing in the Norwegian fjords and would really like to go to Hawaii to ride the waves!

now that....

a-ha **said: "We don't want to take away the fans of** *Duran Duran*... **they need them themselves!"**

All of *a-ha* **prefer to have girlfriends who aren't in any way associated with the pop world because it means that then they can get some kind of rest from having to talk about work!**

Mags is a real car freak and says: "I like all kinds of power sports!"

morten harket of a~ha

Morten Harket is the oldest member of a-ha and was born on 14th September, 1959 in Kongsberg, Norway. He was the second child born into the family, three years after his brother Gunvald.

The numbers soon increased and by the time that he was eight years old he also had a couple of other brothers, and a sister. It was a strong middle class upbringing with their father following the profession of doctor and hoping that some of his children might follow him into that area of work!

"In fact Gunvald did," says Morten, "and I'm always being asked if I'd like to be a doctor too. It's certainly a rewarding thing to do, but at the moment music is what occupies me the most."

Since he didn't live in the capital as Pal and Mags did, his own musical influences were more direct. "I suppose that classical music played a huge part in my early life," he says.

"I was brought up, like all of the family to appreciate the finer points of it and I'm pleased that my father did that.

"But what impressed me most as a young kid was brass bands. I was absolutely absorbed and fascinated by them. It wasn't just the sound, but the shiny instruments, the uniforms of the players; just about everything. Once a year in our town there was a special parade to commemorate a major day in Norway. I was always taken along to see it and watch the band and it really excited me.

"I think that this was probably the greatest influence in making me want to learn some kind of instrument. It really impressed me!"

Being in a rural area also encouraged Morten's interest in wildlife and nature. "When I was young it was always a treat to be taken to the forest for a walk," he says, "and even when I got older I would go there by myself and spend hours just wandering along watching birds, flowers and just generally soaking up this feeling of beauty and freedom. They were all kinds of places that you could have picnics in in the fine weather, and it was even beautiful in the winter."

There were also holidays when the Harket family would go to the sea or on trips inland and Morten is forever enthusiastic about the beauty of the Norwegian countryside. He confesses that he would hate to see any of it spoiled by industry. The fact that the population of the country is also small has helped in keeping the environment more or less the same for ages.

"It's really why I love to be able to go back to my home town. I like to make some of those journeys that I did when I was younger; it's comforting to know that a lot of it is just the same. It's also peaceful and I have my roots there." Now that he is internationally famous he finds those opportunities to return to his natural environment even more rewarding.

"I'm close to my family and I like to be able to go there as often as possible. I've a lot of childhood memories there and also possessions." There are also lots of friends who are always interested in knowing just how his life has changed, and as a person he doesn't think that he has.

At school he impressed his teachers with his academic studies and, although interested in music admits that he suddenly felt the urge to go into religion.

"For some reason," he says, "I thought that my calling was to the church. It's difficult to explain to anyone how that

happens. It's just something that occurs and you know that you've got to do something about it."

He did! On leaving school he applied and was accepted for university where he studied as a theology student, sticking out the whole course and obtaining a degree in the subject.

Then for some reason he felt that he couldn't pursue it. "This is not to say I lost any feeling for religion," he says, "just that it didn't all happen in the way that I expected it would." However, even now, he admits that he is a strongly religious person and that it's quite possible that he could go back to it some time in the future.

The desire to go into music became even stronger, but Morten knew that the only way he could pull things together was if he had sufficient funds to buy equipment and provide for all of the other necessary expenses. He didn't exactly take the easiest of jobs to help this, working as a nurse in a mental home.

It was probably the most stressful period that he has ever experienced. "Definitely the most frightening experience of my life," he says, "because the patients in those kind of places are just so unpredictable. One moment they seem okay and the next they can be at you. In fact

there was just such a moment when one patient who had seemed quite friendly and stable suddenly turned on me and I was really scared.

"You also feel so exhausted at the end of the day. It's the constant demand on you that fills you with stress and I really don't think I was capable of continuing in it for ages!" So he didn't mind one bit when the finances he had been trying to build reached such a stage that he could leave and form a proper group. As it happened, he went on to put together a number of bands with exotic names, but none of them made the success that he had been hoping for.

"There wasn't much happening on the Norwegian music scene," he says. "The radio was the only source of music activity that we could pick up on."

Meanwhile his mother had gone into teaching now that all of her children had grown up. Morten didn't encounter too much resistance to his intentions to be a musician. Perhaps because most of the family had successfully gone on to complete further education.

Because of his love of nature and the wild, it seemed a natural progression for him to be interested in art. He would spend quite a lot of his spare time painting and in this he was encouraged by his sister, four years younger than him, who is now a fully fledged artist! "I think that this is something that Pal, Mags and I all have in common," he says.

He also developed a couple of hobbies which have stuck with him to this day. "I love orchids," he says. "There is something so beautiful about them and they are quite difficult to cultivate. I began trying to grow them myself and it proved to be quite successful. There are just so many different varieties. I was so taken with them that I even named one of my bands after a particular species of them.

"Of course, it's difficult for me to keep up with them now that the group has become successful but I try as much as possible."

The other interest which he took to was collecting butterflies. "I could spend hours watching them in the woods near where I lived," he says. "I used to read lots of books about them and try to spot them if I could."

He admits that where humans are concerned he is the type of person who likes to fall in love. And when a-ha made their first video he met a beautiful model he took to. She must have been something special because he confessed: "I've been out with her longer than I have any other girl."

Morten knew the moment that he met Pal and Mags that they could really get something going musically together. "Although when I first heard what they were playing it wasn't particularly commercial," he says. "It was all a bit gloomy." But he was clever enough to realise the potential the three of them could make together in a studio and on stage and so they got to thinking and trying to write some original material in a more commercial style.

Travel, for Morten, has also meant that he can indulge himself with his hobby of photography. If he isn't taking pictures of the natural environment then he'll have plenty of opportunity to shoot the exotic places he'll be visiting as a-ha becomes increasingly in demand around the world. And he is looking forward to taking his camera to the Far East.

For relaxation, he says, "It's nice to be able to go and see a good film. I enjoy those with good strong stories. The directors are important to me too. I think I'd want to watch a film because so and so directed it, rather than because such and such a superstar was starring in it!"

What is certain, is that when Morten does find somewhere permanent to live, he'll probably want a house with a huge garden. He's not the kind of person who likes to be stuck indoors!

the starsigns of a-ha

Obviously Pal and Morten had nothing to do with the fact of when they were born, but in astrological terms they come under the sign of Virgo. So it's interesting to find out just what the subject has to say about these guys.

Well, for a start, the astrologers say that their wisdom is obtained from experience. No-one would ever try to deny that these guys have gone through that period in their lives when they tried to get as much experience of their business as they could. They were tough times for them, but everyone can now see just how much it paid off. Not many pop stars enter the millionaire status after just one record.

Their starsign also dictates that they love to do everything carefully with great attention to detail. Pal certainly achieves that with his song-writing since he is the principal composer of the group. You can't imagine him just sitting down and bashing out any old thing. He is more the kind of person who likes to try and iron out every possible flaw before he is ready to play his songs to the world.

Their success shows that the Virgo trait pays off in this respect. They're also hard workers and Morten knows all about that from the perseverance of working in the mental institution for a while. That took some strength and determination. But as members of *a-ha* both Morten and Pal show that they stick with it and don't ever give in, whatever the odds are against them!

Astrologers also say that the Virgo type of personality is also strong enough to say 'no'. They don't like to have too many demands made of them, and aren't really afraid to hold their hands up and say 'no'. *a-ha* certainly haven't compromised their music, and there were probably plenty of people who tried to make them be even more commercial than they wanted, with their sounds.

The decision to become more commercial came from them, and no-one else. That's why for years they played the music they wanted to play and the future is about to show that they'll continue to play what they want, although with a world market now in mind rather than the Norwegian club scene!

It's said that Virgos are often workaholics in the sense that they can become insular about it, and find it difficult when they meet people to talk about anything else, or even have any outside interests. But whilst any modern pop group obviously has a lot of pressures placed upon it, with interviews, recordings, touring and so on, Pal and Morten don't seem to be trapped into this Virgo flaw. They manage to sustain a variety of interests outside of their work, and know when to take holidays to relax.

It's curious that astrology says that Virgos can often become good scholars. Look at Morten! He went all the way with his theological studies and is still highly academically inclined, and his family also depict this trait. And there's no doubt that if Pal had not wanted to do music then he too might have ended up in some form of scientific research, following in his father's footsteps.

Virgos, although it's probably true for a lot of other signs too, shouldn't worry too

much. Pal does confess that he bothers a lot about some of the hassles that occur during touring. But then he is also sensible enough to realise that these trivial things are only counterproductive. So he's on the right course for success!

Perfection for Virgos extend into every area, from what they eat, what they wear and where they go. That seems a fair assessment for Pal and Morten. For whilst there were obviously times when they were penniless, whilst trying to make it in the music business, it didn't mean that they didn't recognise what they wanted. The good life is not the sole purpose of the Virgo, rather, they would like to have the best of everything just because that symbolises perfection.

Since they like to be perfect in everything that they do themselves, they like everything else in their lives, no matter how small, to be perfect too!

Mags is a whole different kettle of fish! He's a Scorpio... and Scorpios have the sting in the tail. That means that from out of nowhere something can suddenly inspire them to be pretty angry. But it's usually about something worthwhile. In Mags' case he says that intolerance is perhaps one of the things that gets his wrath up more than most things.

Like Pal and Morten, he wants to do everything perfectly. So the future for *a-ha* looks good. Standing up to the 'baddies' seems to be typical of Scorpios. If there's any kind of injustice going on, they'll fight for the right side! Not violently, but verbally!

Scorpios aren't tactless, but they do speak their mind and aren't afraid to tell the truth. In fact they find it difficult to tell someone otherwise. That can be the sting in the tail too!

They also have strong personalities and draw people to them. Well, Mags certainly can do that. One look at him can tell any fan that!

Scorpios are also not short on sexiness, so Mags fits the bill perfectly!

All things considered, *a-ha* look well suited to each other, maybe the stars brought them together. But they're superstars in their own right now!

a-ha

magne furuholmen of a-ha

Magne Furuholmen, better known as Mags, was born in Oslo, Norway on 1st November, 1962. He ruled the roost at home for about four years until his sister was born. But then disaster struck the family a little while later, when a 'plane carrying his father crashed leaving Mags' mother to bring up her couple of children.

Since his father used to work as a musician he would now have been proud to see the achievements that his son has made with a-ha.

Despite his good looks, Mags comes across as being, perhaps, the most thoughtful member of the group. Although, according to Pal, he is also the most mischievous.

Music was a part of Mags'

life from an early age, even as a kid. He was a member of the school band and frequently performed with them at concerts and in parades. They make a big thing of this in Norway! But it was pop music that eventually grabbed his attention and by the time he was about ten years old, he was already planning on forming a group with his best friend, Pal.

"We knew then that some day we would be famous," he laughs. "Nobody believed us. They thought it was all daydreaming and treated it as a bit of a joke. But we were completely honest about it. That first band was called Spider Empire." Of course, at that age, they weren't into playing gigs and it was more of an after school and weekend activity for the guys.

From then on, they formed a whole string of groups with different people playing in them, as they became more and more inspired by bands like The Doors. "We didn't think in terms of being commercial," he says. "We just wanted to play the things we really wanted to. We weren't trying to please anyone but ourselves. The idea of becoming more commercial with our music came much later."

Like the rest of the band Mags is interested in art and takes quite an academic fascination with it too. He says that his favourite artist is Edward Munch. "I like him," he has said, "because his work is full of passion."

Of all the band he is the one who is most into sporting activities, and if they involve water, then so much the better. His favourite sport is surfing, although he is going to find it difficult to manage to find the time, as the band become even more successful, to do it. But he is hoping to be able to do some when the band visit Australia or other suitable countries.

He agrees that the band has had its personal differences but that they've known each other far too long now to let any problems get in their way. They've tried so hard to become successful that they aren't about to let any disagreements get in their way. And, besides, most of their personal problems were really the result of the awful conditions that they had to live in whilst trying to get a

recording contract for themselves.

As it happens, Mags worked at the same mental institution that Morten did. "He worked there for a much longer period then I did. How he stuck it I don't know. But that was where we met.

"We didn't just become friends and say 'let's form a band.' It was a case of us both talking about music and finding that we had similar tastes and things like that!"

Whilst not saying that he is a superfan of the legendary Bruce Springsteen, he does confess that he quite likes some of his songs and that he admires the way that he can manage to do such lengthy concerts.

All of the band agree that Norway might be thin on the ground musically, but they don't necessarily appreciate the way that so many people put Norway down as a country just because of it.

"Norway is a beautiful place to live and there is so much marvellous scenery there. It's also a lot warmer than people think it is. A nice clean fresh air environment. We all like going back there when we can!"

Mags says that people seem to think that a-ha are another Duran Duran or Wham! but this is not true. "We had to produce a commercial song to begin with, because there wouldn't have been much chance of getting into the charts if we hadn't done that. But it would be wrong for people to assume that this is the only kind of thing that we can do."

Once the band are established, the fans might be surprised to find that there's a lot more to the music of a-ha than they had thought. And this is going to be a pleasant surprise!

Mags admits that he and the others enjoy making the videos and working with some of the real major names in that field. And if they continue to get the attention they did from their first video with the new ones, then their audiences and fans around the world can only increase!

When he isn't working, which is unusual these days, Mags likes to go to the films; usually thought provoking ones rather than science fiction or comedy. Although he does enjoy a good laugh as both Pal and Morten well know!

the
a~ha
quiz

**Here's a chance for you to test
your knowledge of *a-ha*.
Do you think
that you're a super fan?**

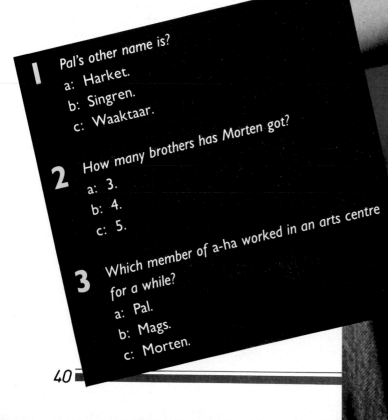

1 Pal's other name is?
  a: Harket.
  b: Singren.
  c: Waaktaar.

2 How many brothers has Morten got?
  a: 3.
  b: 4.
  c: 5.

3 Which member of a-ha worked in an arts centre for a while?
  a: Pal.
  b: Mags.
  c: Morten.

4 Who was called Popeye at school?
   a: Mags.
   b: Pal.
   c: Morten.

5 Who worked on their first video for Take On Me?
   a: Steven Spielberg.
   b: Godley and Creme.
   c: Steve Barron.

6 Where was Morten born?
   a: Oslo.
   b: Kongsberg.
   c: Bergen.

7 Which member of a-ha didn't come on the first trip to London?
   a: Pal.
   b: Morten.
   c: Mags.

8 Mags' favourite sport is what?
   a: Jogging.
   b: Windsurfing.
   c: Tennis.

9 Morten once thought he might become..?
   a: A teacher.
   b: A priest.
   c: A computer programmer.

10 Which year did a-ha come to London for the second time?
   a: 1983.
   b: 1984.
   c: 1985.

11 a-ha's debut single Take On Me was released how many times?
  a: Once.
  b: Twice.
  c: Three times.

12 Pal and Mags once recorded an album in Norway when they had another band. What was the name of the group?
  a: Snow Mountain.
  b: Bridges.
  c: The Whizz Kids.

13 Which instrument did Pal play first in a band?
- a: Guitar.
- b: Drums.
- c: Piano.

14 Morten met a girlfriend making the group's first video. What did she do for a living?
- a: Make up.
- b: Model.
- c: Hair stylist.

15 a-ha's single, Take On Me reached which position in the American charts?
- a: Number 3.
- b: Number 1.
- c: Number 4.

16 In what year did a-ha come together as a group?
- a: 1981.
- b: 1982.
- c: 1983.

17 Who was the last member to join the group?
- a: Morten.
- b: Pal.
- c: Mags.

18 Mags' favourite clothes are?
- a: Leather.
- b: Denim.
- c: Silk.

19 Pal's sister's name is?
- a: Ingrid.
- b: Tongje.
- c: Mai.

20 Mags' favourite film director is?
- a: Spielberg.
- b: Hitchcock.
- c: Kubrick.

21 Who likes orchids?
- a: Pal.
- b: Morten.
- c: Mags.

Answers on page 61.

pal Waaktaar of a-ha

P al Waaktaar was born on the 6th September, 1961 in an Oslo suburb called Manglerud of what could be described as 'middle class' parents. Even today, both of them hold responsible jobs, his father being connected with medical research and his mother as an administrator.

He wasn't the first child to be born into the family as there was already a sister, Tongje, who was a year old when he arrived on the scene. But whilst most sisters might look down on a younger brother, Pal was fortunate in that he had one who helped him and, in later years, supported his ideas.

As can probably be expected, the musical influences to which he was subjected in those early years were not the typical pop charts or rock 'n' roll, despite the fact that the family lived close to the centre of the capital.

"What it did mean," he says, "is that we had immediate access to the theatres and concert halls, so we frequently went to them,

as I was growing up."

However, those concerts were not of the imported rock giants from America and Britain, even though there was a steady flow of musicians into Scandinavia since the mid-1960s.

"The kind of music which was played in our house was frequently of the operatic kind," he says. "And, in a way, I'm pleased about that because it did give me a broader appreciation of music." The outings to the theatre were also to companies producing the major operas or, sometimes a 'treat' would be a visit to the ballet. "I enjoyed it," he says. "I didn't feel as if I was going under sufference!"

Pal says that he has no difficulty in remembering the first record which he bought from an Oslo record shop.

"It was an album of the opera, *Carmen* by Bizet." He says that he always liked this particular one because it wasn't heavy, had a lot of humour in it, and the stage production itself was colourful.

"From that I graduated up a bit," he says, "to the musical *Hair*. I just played it over and over again when I bought it and probably drove everyone crazy. But it was just so different."

Pal progressed musically towards rock quite quickly after this, and when he was ten years old, he came in touch with another boy called Magne who, he discovered, shared the same kind of musical interests as he did. "By now, via the radio and so on, I was fascinated by some of the American and British bands.

"Both Mags and I found that we liked *The Doors*, and also *Deep Purple*. There was nothing like this in Norway. In fact the music scene was particularly stale. You have to appreciate that Norway is not a heavily populated country and that there are a lot of rural industries, fishing and things like that. "It's not a collection of huge cities or metropolises where hundreds of bands are thriving."

The music tended to be 'samey' and middle of the road and Norwegian bands were hardly ever heard outside of their own country. There were a few bands in Oslo who were trying to imitate the American or British sounds, but it was nothing spectacular and the

recording industry was hardly a flourishing activity like it was in many other European countries.

So Pal and Mags would frequently visit each others

houses to play their latest album purchases and knew even then that maybe they would like to some day get a band of their own together. Surprisingly, none of the

guys in the band now say that *The Beatles* influenced them, when practically every other band in the world claims to have been touched at least once by their sounds.

It might well have been this that made Pal and his friend Mags so different in their approaches to music.

At home, his parents didn't look on his later

aspirations to be a musician or pop star as anything more than a mild flirtation. "They weren't negative about it," he says, "but on the other hand they weren't 100%

do in my spare time whilst I did work in a proper job and built a career for myself."

In fact, it was his sister who stood by him through those periods of frustration

listened to him, was always there to confide in and helped coax his parents around to the idea that Pal had to try and make a go of it!

They should have had some idea that he was not really trying for any 'proper' job when he took a succession of rough jobs to help raise money for equipment.

"I hated all of them, but I had to do something to get some money. So I did awful things like scrubbing floors. And on one occasion I even sold tickets on the subway. Along with a string of other hard work which wouldn't lead him anywhere other than to be paid for a week's efforts, he just drifted. He knew that he couldn't put his heart and soul into this kind of work. The only thing that occupied his mind was music and when he went home after a hard day's grind he would sit down and try and compose songs.

Another interest which Pal developed during his schooldays was a love of art! This he says, was all down to his teacher who encouraged his work. "It wasn't just a case of doing it at school, either," he says. "I became interested in visiting galleries and understanding art, as well as just drawing and painting."

He says that he often used to spend many hours working on particular pictures. Even today, he still tries to find the time to work on his artistic talents

behind the idea either. I think that in their opinion I just had this enthusiastic interest in music and that even if I formed a band, then it was just going to be something to

when he tried to convince his parents that it was more than just an interest but something which he wanted to commit himself to in an all out effort to succeed. She

and now that the band are able to travel more widely has had the opportunity to visit some of the more prominent European galleries. He was particularly elated when the group went to New York and he had the chance to go to the galleries there.

Reading is another pastime of his and Pal says that he particularly admires the work of Franz Kafka. And now that he'll probably be spending quite a few hours travelling in 'planes and waiting around in airport lounges, he should have plenty of time on his hands to indulge himself. Working so hard at writing songs has somewhat limited his opportunities to read many new books, or re-read old favourites.

Another of Pal's passions is watching television and he was in his element when the group were in America and he had so many different channels to choose from. He has a fairly wide taste in programmes too, from comedy to music, documentaries to films.

Going to the cinema is also an interest, although he confesses that since the group became well known he has not been able to go as much as he would like, and has to keep in touch with what's happening mostly by video releases. Although he says that when he does watch films he likes them to have a bite to them; something that stimulates his mind whatever the story is about.

So far, his favourite film in the horror area is *Psycho* which is a real chiller and he admits to being a fan of the master of suspense, the late Alfred Hitchcock. He also likes the work of the British director, Lindsay Anderson, mentioning, *If* as being one of the best.

Of the current music scene he says that he doesn't see *a-ha* as being like the next *Wham!* or *Duran Duran*. "Of the music around at the moment, I admire a lot of what Bruce Springsteen does," he says. And who wouldn't when the guy does concerts that last for a duration of four hours or more, and is so committed to his faithful audiences around the world.

"I also like a lot of what *U2* have been doing," he says. But he doesn't stretch his likes into many other areas. Perhaps he wants to try and concentrate on developing an *a-ha* sound that is free of most influences.

As for the girls…he is a winner and openly says that he likes 'romancing'. And you can't get more romantic then he did, when he wanted to take a holiday.

a-ha had been sent around the world on so many promotional trips for their records, appearing on television and doing chat shows, giving interviews to newspapers and for radio, that Pal felt he needed a break somewhere totally different from usual holiday spots.

Well, instead of winging his way to some exotic island, Pal rang up his girlfriend and then went and booked a couple of air tickets to North Africa. "It was just somewhere that I'd always wanted to go to," he says. "You read so much about it or see the kind of places there on film that I wanted to experience it all for myself. It was, I'm pleased to say, a completely different culture and lived up to everything I hoped for."

So Pal spent his time watching the camels, visiting the bazaars and shopping around for bargains and sampling the completely different food. He also took quite a few photographs of his holiday travels so that he'd have something to show the rest of the band when he got back home. Even now he says that he wouldn't mind going back there again sometime when he can travel around some more.

It's nice to know that he doesn't just restrict his travelling to group activities. "Hotels can get a bit boring, and when you're touring around you don't get much chance to see anything of the country or the towns you stay in."

As for the band itself, Pal says Mags is the most spontaneous in the band and the one who provides the most laughs. "You can guarantee that if you're feeling a bit low, then Mags will soon bring you out of it!"

magne furuholmen of

a-ha

a week with a~ha

Just what is it like to spend a week with a-ha? Well, if you followed them around you'd soon find out that there isn't much leisure, but a lot of hard work.

"We could wake up to suddenly find we are flying off to Europe," says Morten. And that's exactly what happened recently. The guys do admit that they try and give themselves some time over the weekend to themselves.

"We might do all kinds of things on a Saturday or Sunday," says Pal. "Going round the shops is always a treat. I much prefer to go browsing than get someone else to do it for me, because there's a certain amount of pleasure attached to even window shopping. You haven't even got the crowds to bother with for a start!"

If the band are recording a new single or album, then they would usually be up quite early so that they could be down at the studio by mid-day. The reason that they'll have a bit of a lie-in is because they were probably still recording into the small hours of the morning. "Once you find that things are going well you don't want to just pack up and go home, even if you are feeling tired," they say.

"We might have been going over some awkward bits with a number and suddenly it all falls into place, so we want to try and get it written down, fresh from our minds."

Of course, working so late does mean that they all tend to miss out on some of their favourite television programmes, but now they video them and if they are still wide awake when they get home, watch some of them then, or save them for a dull Sunday afternoon!

All three of the guys live fairly close to each other in their own houses which they've bought. It means that they do have some time to themselves and are not living out of each others pockets like they used to do when they were really hard up and trying to get known!

This does make things a lot easier when the group has to travel abroad. A few days beforehand they would have checked out their passports and any necessary luggage they required. If it's a promotional visit or just a television show they have to do in Europe, then they don't require to take much with them.

A car would arrive early and drive to each house picking up Pal, Morten and Mags and then drive them to the airport. Recently they flew to Germany and France to do interviews.

But if it is America, then things are on a much larger scale. Visas have to be checked out, clothes bought, often as a last minute rush, and a lot of packing to do. Since all of the guys are into photography, they make certain that all of the equipment they want to take with them is safely packed and that they've sufficient film for their purposes.

They would then be driven to Heathrow Airport where they would board a flight for either New York or Los Angeles. Since the flight is quite a long one, the guys like to catch up on some reading and even some of their fan mail to relieve the boredom. At the other end, in say, New York, they are whisked by car,

supplied from the recording company, to their hotel, where they check-in.

Sometimes when they are away it means that they have to do interviews on quite a few radio shows. So the group have to be certain that they have a list of all of the appointments that they have to go to, and someone makes certain that they are always on time.

The interviews can be varied and interesting. On the radio shows it might just be a straight talk between a dee-jay and members of the band, or it might be that a "phone-in" has been arranged. In this case, fans get the chance to put their questions to individual members of the group.

The band could quite possibly do several of these in a day if they were in America because there are just so many different radio stations. In Europe, it might be an appearance on a few selected music shows. But some days, whether they are on promotional visits or not, the group could find themselves having to do many interviews with various newspapers or music press people in a single day.

"It can get a bit tiring, but it's all part of the job," says Pal. The interviews might be set up

so that they are running just one after the other, with only a hurried break for lunch, and it's not unknown for them to do it like this from early morning until five in the afternoon.

Occasionally, the band also have to attend a photo session and this can also take all day. Quite a bit of planning has to go into this, with clothes being chosen and sorted out for the different shots. The group would have to arrive at a photographic studio quite early in order to be made up for the photographer to set up all the correct lighting. Hundreds of photographs might be taken in order to provide a few really good ones which he is satisfied with, and it requires a lot of sitting around and being patient!

Some days, when there are no appointments for them to fulfil, Pal will possibly spend some time working on new songs for the group. Then of course, once these are written the band has to rehearse them.

A lot of rehearsal also has to take place when the band are going to embark on a major tour. The stage act has to be planned meticulously so that it all runs smoothly when they face an audience. And a-ha are the ultimate professionals when it comes to this. Any problems

have to be ironed out before the tour starts.

Once a tour does begin, then a lot of the day is spent travelling from one city to the next. This can involve coach, or 'plane. Once in the town where the venue is to be played, the band check into their hotel and then have to go to the theatre, where their equipment has been set up so that they can do what is called a 'sound check' to make certain that everything is in working order and that no matter where the fans sit in the audience they'll be able to hear everything clearly.

After a concert it can take a long time to wind down from all that excitement, so the guys might go for a quiet meal. Occasionally there could be a party and probably definitely at the end of the tour when all of the road crew and other people who have been travelling with them would celebrate its success!

Making videos can add another dimension to the week. In these cases a couple of days could be involved as a-ha are directed through the film and then have to watch the results during editing.

All things considered, is it any wonder that occasionally Pal, Morten and Mags like to get away for a holiday?!

the quiz~answers

1: c.	8: b.	15: b.
2: a.	9: b.	16: a.
3: b.	10: a.	17: a.
4: b.	11: c.	18: b.
5: c.	12: b.	19: b.
6: b.	13: b.	20: b.
7: b.	14: b.	21: b.

How did you do? If you scored between 15 to 21 then a-ha can be proud of you. You really are up there with the mega-fans of the group. Between 9 and 14 you are certainly in the running to move into the megafan bracket. Bet if you re-did the quiz you'd manage a higher score. And if you scored below 9, don't worry... now you've read the answers you could probably score top marks!